PROTECTING LEOPARDS

Some subspecies of leopards are almost extinct. Zoos are trying to save these leopards. Zookeepers share and trade adult leopards that are ready to have families. The leopards mate and have strong, healthy cubs. Some of these cubs may be set free in wildlife parks. There they can live, hunt, and raise their own families. By setting these leopards free, many people hope to protect the different subspecies of leopards in the world.

◀ Most leopard cubs grow and live to be about twelve years old in the wild. In zoos they can live as long as 23 years.

A FUTURE FOR LEOPARDS

We need to protect the many leopards that still live in the wild. Some subspecies of leopards will become extinct unless something is done to save them. The places where leopards live, such as forests and grasslands, are being taken over by people who want to build farms, roads, cities, and golf courses. Some countries are setting aside land for wildlife parks. But others are doing very little to save leopards.

People must learn that all animals need wild places where they can be safe and free.

GLOSSARY

adaptable (uh-DAP-tuh-bul) When you are able to deal with change.

attract (uh-TRAKT) To draw other people, animals, or things to you.

extinct (eks-TINKT) When there are no living members of a certain species left on Earth.

fierce (FEERS) Strong and ready to fight.

hyena (hy-EE-nuh) A dog-like animal that eats other animals for food.

illegal (il-LEE-gul) Against the law.

jaguar (JA-gwar) One of the four species of great cats.

litter (LIH-ter) A group of baby animals born to the same mother at the same time.

mate (MAYT) A special joining of a male body and female body. After mating, the female may have a baby growing inside her body.

poacher (POH-cher) A person who kills animals that are protected by law.

prey (PRAY) An animal that is eaten by another animal for food.

prowl (PROWL) To move around looking for food.

species (SPEE-sheez) A group of animals that are very much the same.

subspecies (SUB-spee-sheez) A group of animals that are similar but have some differences.

WEB SITES:

You can learn more about leopards on the Internet! Check out this Web site: http://www.primenet.com/~brendel/

23

INDEX

BIG CATS

LEOPARDS

Don Middleton

The Rosen Publishing Group's
PowerKids Press™
New York

This book is dedicated to my wife Sue and my daughters Jody and Kim. Without their support, my writing and other wildlife adventures would not have been possible. Also, a special thanks to author and friend Diana Star Helmer for believing in me.

Published in 1999 by The Rosen Publishing Group, Inc.
29 East 21st Street, New York, NY 10010

First Edition

Book Design: Danielle Primiceri

Photo Credits: Cover © 1997 Digital Vision Ltd.; pp. 4, 8, 19 © Stan Osolinski/FPG International; p. 7 © Bob Jacobson/International Stock; p. 9, 16 © A.Schmidecker/FPG International; p. 10, 14 © Mark Newman/International Stock; p. 13 © Frank Grant/International Stock; p. 20 © Gail Shumway/FPG International; p. 22 © Telegraph Colour Library/FPG International.

MIddleton, Don
    Leopards / Don Middleton.
       p.   cm. — (Big cats)
    Includes index.
    Summary: Discusses the habitat, lifestyle, diet, behavior, and appearance of leopards in Africa and Asia.
    ISBN 0-8239-5209-6
    1. Leopard—Juvenile literature. [1. Leopard.] I. Title. II. Series: Middleton, Don. Big cats.
    QL737.C23M543 1998
    599.75'54—dc21
                                       97-32682
                                              CIP
                                               AC

Manufactured in the United States of America

CONTENTS

A GREAT CAT

Leopards are one of the four **species** (SPEE-sheez) of "great cats." The other species of great cats are tigers, lions, and **jaguars** (JA-gwarz). The four great cats are the only wild cats who can give a mighty roar!

There are more leopards than all of the other great cats combined. And leopards live in more places than any of the other wild cats. Leopards are found in southern Africa, southern Asia, and in China. More than 250,000 leopards may still live in the wild.

Did you know that leopards can hear two times better than people? And in low light, leopards ▶ can see six times better than people!

LOTS OF LEOPARDS

There are more than 25 **subspecies** (SUB-spee-sheez) of leopards. Some subspecies, such as Anatolian leopards, are nearly **extinct** (eks-TINKT). Anatolian leopards live in the countries of Turkey, Syria, and Lebanon. There are also wild cats called snow leopards and clouded leopards. These leopards are a totally different species than the spotted leopards we're talking about. But even though they're not "great cats," they're still called leopards.

Most leopards are almost three feet tall. Their bodies can grow to be six feet long. Leopards have long tails. Male leopards can weigh up to 200 pounds. Females are usually smaller than males.

◀ Leopards look a lot like another great cat: the jaguar. But leopards have longer legs, smaller spots, and a smaller head than jaguars.

A CAT OF MANY COATS

Leopards are beautiful animals. Their fur can be light yellow or dark orange. Some leopards even have all-black fur. All leopards have black spots and rings on their fur. Black leopards have spots too. But it's hard to see the spots because their fur is black. The spots on a leopard's fur blend in with the trees and grass. This helps leopards hide when they are hunting.

A female leopard's fur is usually softer than a male leopard's fur. ▶

▼

Sometimes black leopards are called black panthers. Cubs with black fur and cubs with yellow fur can be born in the same **litter** (LIH-ter).

STRONG AND FIERCE

Leopards are strong and **fierce** (FEERS) hunters. They hide in trees and hunt monkeys and baboons. In the forest a leopard will sneak up very close to its **prey** (PRAY). The leopard then springs from its hiding place. It uses its strong body and sharp claws to hold the animal. It kills its prey by biting the animal's throat. The leopard then carries its prey high up into a tree before eating it. This keeps lions, **hyenas** (hy-EE-nuhz), and wild dogs from stealing it.

◀ Leopards are strong enough to carry prey that is bigger than they are into trees that are as high as 30 feet!

SECRET LIVES

Leopards live in forests, grasslands, swamps, mountains, and desert-like areas. Some even live close to towns and large cities. This makes leopards the most **adaptable** (uh-DAP-tuh-bul) of all the big cats. Except for mothers with cubs, leopards like to live alone.

Leopards do not like to be seen by people. If there are lots of people around, leopards will hunt at night. Resting or sleeping leopards can usually be found deep in the forest or high up in the branches of a large tree.

Trees are a leopard's favorite place to hang out. ▶

Baby leopards can walk when they are thirteen days old. They start to follow their mom around when they are about three months old.

▼

ear only a few people are attacked and killed by
s. However, many years ago in the Panar district
, one leopard killed almost 400 men, women,
ldren! Hunters finally found the leopard and had
it to protect the people.

ds are on the **prowl** (PROWL) at night. So in
where leopards live, people are warned to stay
heir homes when it is dark. This keeps people safe
ngry leopards. But leopards are not always safe
ople. Every year, people called **poachers** (POH-
ill thousands of leopards **illegally** (il-LEE-gul-lee) for
n, claws, teeth, and other body parts.

Leopards usually hunt at sunrise and sunset.
This is when they are least likely to be ▶
seen by people or by their prey.

BABY LEOPARDS

When a female leopard is ready to **mate** (MAYT), she
leaves a special smell on the ground. This **attracts** (uh-
TRAKTS) a male leopard. After mating, the male
leaves. Three to four months later the female gives birth
to two or three cubs. The leopard cubs each
weigh about three pounds. That is about
half the weight of a human baby.

At birth leopard cubs are blind and
helpless. The mother leopard hides
the cubs in a cave or some
other safe, secret place. The little
cubs spend their time drinking their
mother's milk or sleeping next to
each other.

GROWING UP

When leopard cubs are about three
begin to travel with their mother wh
cubs watch their mother closely. The
animals are good to eat. They also
them. At first the cubs practice by sr
other. Then they begin to hunt frogs,
small animals. When they are two y
leave their mother to live alone in th

Leopard mothers teach their cubs everything the cub
need to know when they go off to live on their own.

LE

Each y
leopard
of India
and ch
to shod

Leopar
places
inside t
from hu
from pe
cherz)
their sk

18

BABY LEOPARDS

When a female leopard is ready to **mate** (MAYT), she leaves a special smell on the ground. This **attracts** (uh-TRAKTS) a male leopard. After mating, the male leaves. Three to four months later the female gives birth to two or three cubs. The leopard cubs each weigh about three pounds. That is about half the weight of a human baby.

At birth leopard cubs are blind and helpless. The mother leopard hides the cubs in a cave or some other safe, secret place. The little cubs spend their time drinking their mother's milk or sleeping next to each other.

GROWING UP

When leopard cubs are about three months old, they begin to travel with their mother when she hunts. The cubs watch their mother closely. They learn which animals are good to eat. They also learn how to catch them. At first the cubs practice by sneaking up on each other. Then they begin to hunt frogs, lizards, and other small animals. When they are two years old, the cubs leave their mother to live alone in the forest.

◀ Leopard mothers teach their cubs everything the cubs will need to know when they go off to live on their own.

LEOPARDS AND PEOPLE

Each year only a few people are attacked and killed by leopards. However, many years ago in the Panar district of India, one leopard killed almost 400 men, women, and children! Hunters finally found the leopard and had to shoot it to protect the people.

Leopards are on the **prowl** (PROWL) at night. So in places where leopards live, people are warned to stay inside their homes when it is dark. This keeps people safe from hungry leopards. But leopards are not always safe from people. Every year, people called **poachers** (POH-cherz) kill thousands of leopards **illegally** (il-LEE-gul-lee) for their skin, claws, teeth, and other body parts.

Leopards usually hunt at sunrise and sunset. This is when they are least likely to be ▶ seen by people or by their prey.